# THE GANGES

written and photographed by

## David Cumming

RSVP

**RAINTREE**
**STECK-VAUGHN**
P U B L I S H E R S
The Steck-Vaughn Company

*Austin, Texas*

**Cover** *Pilgrims gather at one of the main ghats
at Varanasi for a ritual bath in the Ganges, the
river they believe to be holy.*

**Series and book editor** Rosemary Ashley
**Series designer** Derek Lee
**Book designer** Paul Bennett

**Library of Congress Cataloging-in Publishing Data**

Cumming, David, 1953-
    The Ganges / David Cumming.
      p.    cm. — (Rivers of the world)
    Includes index.
    Summary: An overview of the Ganges River, one of the largest
waterways in the world, valued not only for trade and irrigation,
but for its religious importance to Hindus.
    ISBN 0-8114-3105-3
    1. Ganges River (India and Bangladesh)—Juvenile literature.
2.Ganges Valley—Description and travel—Juvenile literature.
I. Title.   II. Series.
    DS485.G25C86   1994
    954'.1'009693--dc20                         93-11987
                                                    CIP
                                                     AC

Typeset by Multifacit Graphics, Keyport, NJ
Printed in Italy by G. Canale & C.S.p.A., Turin
Bound in the United States by Lake Book, Melrose Park, IL
1 2 3 4 5 6 7 8 9 0 LB 99 98 97 96 95 94

# RIVERS OF THE WORLD

The Amazon
The Ganges
The Mississippi
The Nile
The Rhine
The Thames

# CONTENTS

# 1
# "Mother Ganges"

*"The Ganga, especially, is the river of India, beloved of her people, round which are intertwined her memories, her hopes and fears, her songs of triumph, her victories and her defeats. She has been a symbol of India's age-long culture and civilization, ever changing, ever flowing and yet ever the same Ganga."*
*Jawaharlal Nehru, Prime Minister of India (1947–1964)*

The Ganges is unique. Not because of the river's amazing length or width or other unusual features. Other rivers surpass the Ganges on most of these counts. But no other river can match the reverence and affection that is shown to the Ganges by the people of India. These feelings are reflected in the thousand names given to the river. In addition to its proper Indian name, Ganga, other names include *Sughosha* (meaning "the melodious"), *Bhagya-janani* ("the creator of happiness"), *Jagada-hita* ("the friend of all that lives and moves") and, perhaps the most telling of all, *Ganga mai* (Mother Ganges), the giver of life.

A village in Bangladesh, in the Ganges delta region.

Approximately 300 million people, more than all the population of the United States, live in the Ganges river basin: 200 million live on the northern plains of India and another 100 million in the delta shared with neighboring Bangladesh. People are dependent on the Ganges for water and food.

The Ganges also enriches the spiritual lives of millions of Hindus, for whom the river is holy because they believe it is the goddess Ganga come to earth. For this reason, the river is thought of as female and is always referred to as "she" or "her." Hindus worship the river as they would any god or goddess of their religion, Hinduism. Many Hindus want their ashes disposed in the Ganges.

Holy and vital for their survival it may be, but this has not stopped people from abusing the river. Today, the poisonous wastes from homes and factories are choking the Ganges, changing a source of fresh water into a sewer—turning a source of life into a destroyer of life. Deforestation, too, has

**Facts and Figures about the Ganges River**
Source: The Gangotri glacier, 15 miles long by 5 miles wide, located at a height of 13,970 feet in the Himalaya Mountains of north eastern India. Delta area: 80,600 sq. miles shared by India and Bangladesh, on the northern coast of the Bay of Bengal, in the Indian Ocean.
Length: 1,550 miles
Area of Basin: 722,610 sq. miles

blocked the river with soil washed off the highlands. Many believe an angry Mother Ganges regularly bursts her banks after the monsoon rains to take revenge on selfish, uncaring humans.

Even if the people are not worried, the Indian government most certainly is. The government is so concerned about the state of the river that it has set up the Ganges Action Plan to clean it. Now India can look forward to a revitalized Ganges: a Ganges which it is hoped will also provide huge amounts of electricity, as well as much-needed water for the drier southern regions of India.

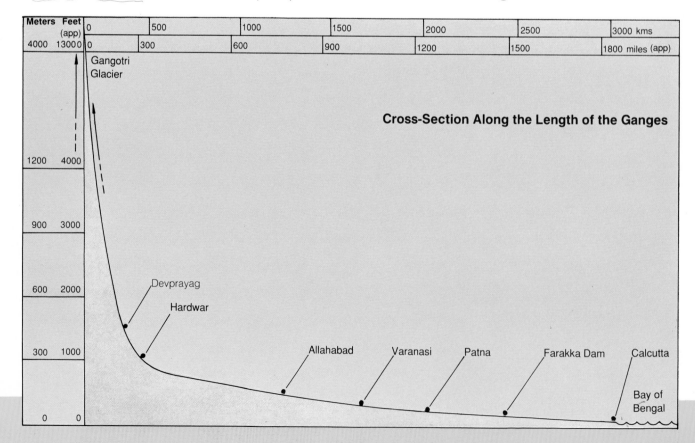

Cross-Section Along the Length of the Ganges

### The upper Ganges

Most people consider the true source of the Ganges to be the meltwaters of the Gangotri glacier, 13,970 feet up in the Himalaya Mountains. The powerful little river created by the thawing ice is called the Bhagirathi. Some 124 miles downstream it is joined by the Alaknanda and their combined waters become known as the Ganges River.

At this point, the Ganges is a typical mountain torrent, using the power produced by its steep fall to the plains to carve a narrow channel through the rock, squirming through narrow gorges and thundering over innumerable rapids. After plunging nearly 12,477 feet in the first 310 miles, the Ganges reaches the plains at Hardwar. From here onward, it descends to sea level at a slower pace, dropping 985 feet in the next 1,178 miles

The Bhagirathi (left) and Alaknanda rivers merge to become the Ganges at the town of Devprayag.

### How the Himalayas Were Formed

India and Asia have not always been joined together. Originally, they were separated by a sea, into which flowed two large rivers, the present-day Indus and Brahmaputra, and many smaller ones. All the sediment brought down by them gradually built up in layers on the seabed.

Then, about 25 million years ago, enormous forces within the earth's crust began pulling India and Asia together. When they collided, all the layers of sediment in the sea were crushed and squeezed upward, forming the "fold mountains" known today as the Himalayas (*right*). The Ganges was one of the rivers created after the appearance of the Himalayas.

India and Asia are still being pulled toward each other, not smoothly, but in sudden jerks that can cause earthquakes. Some of the most powerful and destructive earthquakes in the world have occurred among the Himalayas. In October 1991, for example, 1,000 people died in an earthquake, just north of Hardwar.

to its wide delta in the Bay of Bengal.

The Ganges has helped to develop these plains, not merely by depositing another layer of topsoil when it floods its banks every summer, but also by providing the land with water for irrigation. Nowhere is this vital role more noticeable than at Hardwar, where much of the water is diverted by a dam into the Upper Ganges Canal, reducing the river to little more than a tributary. The dam also produces hydroelectricity. When it was constructed, in 1854, the canal was the largest irrigation system in the world, supplying 1,500,525 acres of farmland. The Ganges only becomes a major river again at Allahabad, where it is joined by the Yamuna.

The Ganges at Hardwar, at the start of its long journey across the plains. The river curves away in the background. In the foreground is the Upper Ganges Canal.

This impressive, modern suspension bridge joins the river's two banks at Rishikesh, in the foothills of the Himalayas.

## The middle Ganges

During this stage of its course, from Allahabad to Patna, the Ganges gradually grows in size, swollen by the waters of the Yamuna. But it remains only a medium-sized river the length of its journey through the state of Uttar Pradesh.

Soon after the city of Varanasi, the Ganges enters the state of Bihar and takes on the character of a major river. Broad and filled with sediment from several large tributaries, including the Ghaghara, Gandak, and Son, it

meanders sluggishly across the huge flat plain. At this point the river is unpredictable in behavior—dozing for most of the year, then alarmingly destructive: one year washing away farmland, the next, shifting course to provide more land. The Ganges' plain is littered with cities once on the river's banks, but now no longer occupied. Rajmahal, on the borders of the states of Bihar and West Bengal, was deserted in the early 1860s when the Ganges moved 3 miles away. Ten years later, the river was 6 miles away. Today Rajmahal is a mere ghost town.

### How the Ganges' Plain Was Formed

In geological terms, the Himalayas are young, so their rocks are still soft and easily eroded by the monsoon rains: more than 1,000 tons of rock are worn away from each square mile every year. After the formation of the Himalayas, there was a deep valley between them and the Deccan, as the highlands of southern India are called. Over millions of years, this valley was filled up with all the rocky sediment washed off the mountains, to form a huge flat plain 198 miles wide, over which the Ganges flows to the sea.

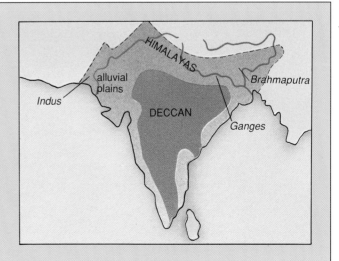

Today it is hard to imagine that this part of the Ganges was once a busy commercial waterway linking the Bay of Bengal with the central plains. Two hundred years ago the river was navigable all year round, so in 1794 the East India Company began operating a regular paddle-steamer service between Calcutta and Allahabad. Late in the following century, it had to be closed down because the river had become too shallow for the ships—it was difficult even to reach Patna. The Upper Ganges Canal had robbed the river of much of its water, and deforestation of the highland areas had filled the Ganges and its tributaries with large amounts of silt.

**Right** Hanging out the wash after a day spent ferrying people across the river.

**Below** Pilgrims' boats at the point where the Ganges and Yamuna meet at Allahabad.

## The lower Ganges

Beyond Patna the dry plains of Bihar give way to the wetlands of West Bengal, the last Indian state in the Ganges' journey to the sea. The main river continues on into Bangladesh, where it unites with the Brahmaputra River to become the Padma River before continuing into the Bay of Bengal. Meanwhile, a tributary, confusingly called the Bhagirathi again, heads directly south to join the Hooghly River and they then flow into the Bay of Bengal. This was the main exit of the Ganges until the twelfth century, when the land tilted, draining the water out of the Bhagirathi and into the Padma.

**Below** There are few roads and no railroads in the Sundarbans so boats are the main form of transportation.

**Above** The trees that cover most of the muddy islands in the Sundarbans are often almost submerged by the high levels of water.

The Hooghly and the Padma rivers share an enormous delta, 80,600 square miles in size. At its ragged edge, where the land fans out into the sea, forming more than fifty muddy islands that are separated by a maze of channels, there is the world's largest estuarine (river mouth) forest: 16,120 square miles of mangrove trees. This is the Sundarbans, so called because of the sundari trees that once grew here in abundance. The trees have been cut down for housing and boat building or killed by the increased salinity of the water.

11

Sagar Island, at the mouth of the Hooghly, is traditionally the place where the Ganges ends its journey, emptying into the Bay of Bengal with such force that its sludgy waters can be seen 372 miles out in the ocean.

**Opposite** Villagers wash in one of the many channels of the Ganges delta.

### Wildlife in the Ganges' Basin

The Ganges' plains were once covered in dense forests, full of wild animals. As the forests were cut down, the animals retreated to the highland forests. Even here the tiger, elephant, and musk deer have not been safe from hunters after their skins, their tusks for ivory or, in the case of musk deer, the scent glands used in perfumes. Animal numbers have declined so much that special conservation parks have been opened where they can live in safety.

Other animals living in the forests include bears, leopards, foxes, jackals, boars, and monkeys, as well as snakes and monitor lizards. In the air, you can see more than 500 species of birds, from parakeets and kingfishers to storks and woodpeckers.

There are many varieties of fish in the Ganges' waters, including salmon and trout. The river is famous for crocodiles *(see below)* and the closely related gavial, with its distinctive long, thin snout. The gavial eats only fish, whereas the crocodile will also consume human and animal flesh.

In the Sundarbans the Bengal tiger is equally at home on land as in water.

## The Sundarbans

The Sundarbans is a unique water environment where plants and animals are continuously adapting to a habitat that has a daily cycle of high and low tides, bringing in and then flushing out large quantities of nutrients. Eighty percent of the land is under water at high tide. The Sundarbans is situated at the meeting point of sea and river water and the slightest change in the flow alters the salinity of the water. This affects plants, and later on, the animals that feed on them.

The tiger is an interesting example of how a species has been forced to adapt to an ever-changing environment. Here, a tiger is equally at home on dry land and in the water. It is also capable of swimming up to 6 miles between islands in search of prey. It is not fussy whether it dines on seafood—fish, crab, or turtle—or on a land-based deer, monitor lizard, wild boar, or even the occasional human. Of the 300 Bengal tigers in the Sundarbans, about 60 are man-eaters; in 1991 they killed 32 people.

The trees, too, which spend half their lives almost afloat, have developed long, drooping root systems to anchor themselves in the ground. Some even have roots that poke up through the mud at low tide to take in air.

# 3
# Weather and Climate

## The three seasons

There are three distinct seasons in northern India and Bangladesh. The winter months, from November to February, are mild and dry: daytime temperatures do not go above 76° F and the rainfall is less than 1 inch a month. Spring, from March to May, is very hot and dry: the rainfall remains low, but temperatures soar to 104° F. The summer months, from June to October, are hot and very wet: temperatures drop a little and the rainfall is heavy. In July more than 16 inches of rain falls in the Himalayan foothills and delta, and 12 inches on the plains.

Each year, during the monsoon season, huge areas of Bangladesh are flooded.

## The monsoon

The rain is brought by the winds, called the monsoon, that sweep across the Indian Ocean from the southwest, reaching the tip of India at the end of May. The increase in temperatures during the spring heats up the land more quickly than the water in the surrounding sea. As the land gets warmer, so the air above it becomes hotter and rises, causing a decrease in the air pressure. Out to sea, the pressure remains higher above the cooler water. By the end of May, the difference in pressure between the two is so great that air is literally sucked inland. As the winds are dragged over the ocean, they pick up moisture, which is dropped as rain on the parched land.

The monsoon winds that pass to the south of India bend left and head up the east coast toward Calcutta, where they split into two streams. The right-hand stream of the monsoon branches off northeastward, to drop its rain on Bangladesh. The left one turns up the valley of the Ganges. The further west the winds travel, the drier it becomes, so that farmers on the plains of the upper Ganges receive much less rain than those in West Bengal. West Bengal and Bangladesh are the wettest areas; the central regions of the states of Bihar and

## Some Monsoon Facts

The following information shows how the monsoon affects the lives of the people of India and Bangladesh.

- The monsoon brings 80 percent of Bangladesh's yearly rainfall.
- Nearly 60 percent of Bangladesh's rice is grown during the monsoon season.
- Most of Bangladesh is flat and very low, no more than 15 feet above sea level. In a good year, only 20 percent of the land is flooded during the monsoon; in a bad year, 80 percent is flooded.
- The Ganges, reduced to just a trickle in many parts during the dry winter months, comes alive after the monsoon, often with terrible consequences. In 1982, in Uttar Pradesh state, 15,000 houses were destroyed and 2,000 villages cut off, as, swollen by the rains, the Ganges eroded its banks and shifted its course, flooding nearby land.
- If the monsoon fails (as it last did in 1987) and only a little rain comes, it has been estimated that 15 million Indians are put out of work because their jobs rely on agriculture.
- In the summer of 1877, 5 million Indians starved to death when the monsoon rains did not arrive; a century earlier, 10 million perished in a famine in Bengal.
- Indian meteorologists report that monsoon failures have become more frequent in the last twenty years: 1987 was the ninth year in a decade when the monsoon failed to bring rain to northern India. Fortunately, India is better able today to deal with a drought: weather satellites provide advance warning so that wells can be dug and plans made to distribute food.

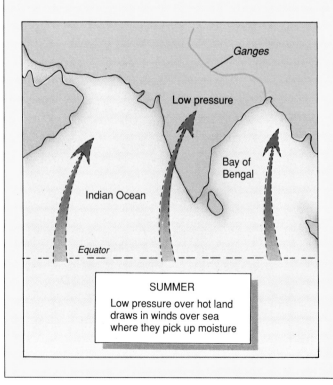

SUMMER
Low pressure over hot land draws in winds over sea where they pick up moisture

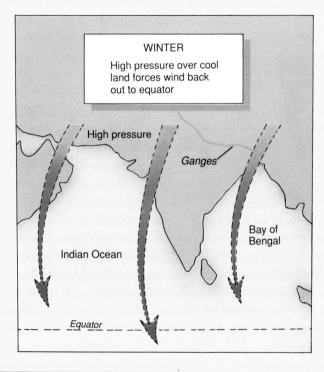

WINTER
High pressure over cool land forces wind back out to equator

Uttar Pradesh are the driest. In some years, there is so little rain here that there have been droughts and terrible famines and millions of people have died.

People cannot rely on the amount of rain the monsoon will bring. In some years, it is only a small amount and farmers' crops can be ruined. In other years, it can be too much and villages and cities are flooded with deep water.

Fierce storms at the end of the summer are powerful enough to lift huge ships out of the river. This ship has been stranded near Dacca.

Raised banks protect villages in the Sundarbans from high water levels in the delta's channels.

## Cyclones and surges

At the end of September, as the temperature drops and the land cools, the air pressure above it rises, forcing the monsoon winds back out to sea. As they retreat southward to the equator, fierce storms, called cyclones, are stirred up over the Bay of Bengal and lash the coasts of Bangladesh and east India. Strong winds funnel the sea into the shallow, narrow channels of the Ganges' delta, creating a huge surge of water, frequently more than 13 feet high and topped with waves equally tall. This massive wall of water tumbles over the

### Mobarak Ullah Mazumder

"I am the captain of the paddle-steamer Ghazi which travels from Dacca to Khulna and back again, along the waterways of the Ganges' delta in Bangladesh. The 403-mile round trip can only be done during the dry season, when the channel markers and river banks can be clearly seen. It is too risky in the wet summer months because the water rises so high that most of the markers and banks are hidden. Even though we carry a pilot who knows the channels, the Ghazi often runs aground."

## The Effects of Global Warming on Bangladesh

If scientists are correct about global warming there could be a catastrophe in Bangladesh. Most of the country is so low-lying that even a small rise in the level of the oceans could have devastating consequences, drowning many people and flooding thousands of acres of land. Weather scientists are also worried that global warming will increase the power of cyclones, making them even more destructive in years to come.

These houses in Bangladesh are built on stilts to protect them from floods.

low, unprotected islands of the delta, destroying and sweeping away everything in its path. A particularly bad cyclone devastated Bangladesh in November 1970, when winds of more than 124 mph and a 26-foot high surge killed 300,000 people, left one million homeless, drowned half a million cattle, and washed away most of the rice crop and the country's fishing boats.

Rice paddy fields in the low-lying lands of the delta are often flooded during the monsoon season.

# 4
# Agriculture

## The effects of weather and terrain

Subsistence farming is the main type of agriculture on the Ganges' plains and delta. This means that the farmers are able to cultivate enough food for their own needs, to feed their families, but not enough to sell for an income.

Rainfall is the biggest problem for farmers—not just how much, but when it falls. Little rain falls during the winter months from November to May; most comes in the summer, brought by the monsoon.

In the highland areas, where there is snow and ice in winter, both farmers and their crops are affected by the freezing temperatures. Down on the plains, the very hot summer temperatures mean that farmers have to do all their work early in the mornings and evenings, resting at home in the blisteringly hot afternoons.

The plains and the delta are very flat so they are easily farmed, with bullocks being used to plow the soil. The steep-sided valleys of the mountains and foothills are much more difficult to plow

Terraced farmland on the steep slopes of the Alaknanda valley in the Himalayas.

and there all the work has to be done by hand. The land has to be terraced to prevent the soil from being washed away by the rain. But although the soil is thin and stony, a wide variety of crops are cultivated, including fruits (apples, oranges, and lemons), wheat, vegetables, (tomatoes, cauliflowers, and cabbages), and even some tea. On the lowlands, the deep, rich alluvium, washed down by the rivers, is ideal for growing many types of crops.

**Right** Few farmers in India can afford modern machines to help them in their work.

**Fertile Soil**
The sediment brought down from the mountains by the Ganges is ground down to fine particles on its journey to the plain, and mixed up with mud and sand to form alluvium. This is a fertile soil, full of the nutrients plants thrive on, so it is ideal for farming. A new layer of alluvium is brought down from the highlands every year after the snow melts and the monsoon arrives. When rivers flood this fertile soil is spread over new areas.

**Left** Locally grown fruit and vegatables on sale at a shop in a mountain village in the valley of the Alaknanda.

## The crops

Little rain for much of the year means that farmers need to grow two types of crops to get the maximum use from their land: a winter crop that needs only a little rain and a summer crop that needs a lot of rain.

These crops are called *rabi* and *kharif*. *Rabi* crops require lower temperatures and rainfall than *kharif* crops, so they are sown at the end of the rainy season, in October and November. They are harvested in April and May, before the start of the monsoon. *Rabi* crops include wheat, barley, and gram (seed plants similar to beans).

*Kharif* crops need heat and moisture, so they are planted just before the monsoon and harvested when it finishes, in October and November. *Kharif* crops include rice, corn, millets, cotton, and sugarcane.

In the delta region, the farmers can grow only one crop a year, a *kharif* crop which is either rice or jute—both need heavy rain during their growing season. In the dry winter months, the river level is low, so tides penetrate farther upstream in the delta, increasing the water's salinity and making it harmful to use on crops. The farmers lack the pumps needed to draw fresh water from deep underground to irrigate the land. As they are unable to farm, they turn to fishing, gathering honey, or wood-cutting.

Many people earn a living from the rich supplies of fish in the Ganges delta.

**Left** The sandy silt of the riverbed near Kanpur is good for growing fruit and vegetables in the winter. During the monsoon, all this land is flooded as the rains swell the river.

**Right** One of the dams at Hardwar at the beginning of the Upper Ganges Canal. The Canal is used to irrigate land that would otherwise be difficult to farm.

## Irrigation

A long dry season means that a farmer must irrigate his fields to prevent the rabi harvest from being ruined. In the driest areas of the Ganges' plains, canals provide the main form of irrigation. At Hardwar, for instance, a dam diverts much of the river's water into the Upper Ganges Canal, from where smaller channels distribute water among the farmers' fields. Farther downstream, water is supplied by wells. Traditional wells involve using a bucket to draw up water from a deep hole in the ground. Modern wells are tube-wells, where a long plastic tube is sunk into the ground and the water is sucked up by a motor driven pump, powered either by electricity, gasoline, or diesel.

The monsoon can bring too much rain in some years and too little in others. Some years the monsoon arrives on time; other years, it is late. So farmers cannot rely on the monsoon and they must be prepared to irrigate their land even in the summer, especially when the monsoon fails.

## Social and political problems

In India people have large families, and when parents die, land is divided up equally between all the sons of a family. Over the centuries this has meant that farms, which once may have been large and profitable, have been broken up into smaller and smaller units as they have been handed down from one generation to the next. Since most farmers can do no more than feed themselves, they are forced to find other income.

As a consequence, some farmers decide to buy extra land. With no savings, they are usually forced to borrow from a local moneylender, usually at a very high rate of interest. Or they may rent some extra fields, paying the landowner either in cash or with a part of the harvest. Either way, it is very costly and farmers are faced with a crippling debt that is very often passed on to their sons.

This granary was built in 1786 to store food for use in times of famine.

Jute grown in the delta region is taken by boat for sale in Dacca.

24

Bullocks are a common sight in rural India. They are used for pulling carts and also to pull plows across fields.

The plight of the farmer is made worse by the caste system—a rigid division of Hindus into different social groups. Hinduism is the principal religion of India and higher caste Hindus own most of the land while the lowest caste are often landless laborers.

Political factors cause problems for farmers, too. In Western countries, governments have scientists and advisers to help farmers. But in India and Bangladesh there are few of these and money for agricultural research is limited. In the West, too, inexpensive bank loans and government grants are available to farmers who want to expand or invest in new equipment. In India and Bangladesh such financial help is not so easy to obtain. Without such support, the struggle to modernize overwhelms many farmers, and they are forced to continue with their age-old methods.

All this presents a gloomy picture of farming in India and Bangladesh. In reality, though, the situation has improved a great deal since the 1960s, especially in India. But reforms, while benefiting the wealthier farmers and India as a whole, have also done much damage to the millions of small-scale farmers, who make up the bulk of the agricultural system.

This boat is loaded with teak wood for furniture making. Delta farmers earn a lot of money from growing timber.

## The Green Revolution in India

The "Green Revolution" is the phrase used to describe the replacement of many traditional farming methods in developing countries with up-to-date techniques common in Western nations. In India, the revolution started in the late 1960s, when the government began to introduce major changes.

It was decided that there would be a complete shake-up of the agricultural system in India. Chemical fertilizers were imported, along with new types of strong, disease-resistant seeds that yielded larger harvests than the homegrown varieties. Indian scientists began researching into increasing the production of other crops. Bank loans were provided for tractors, machines, fertilizers, and pesticides, and advisers were sent to villages to give information and advice about improving farming techniques.

While all this was happening, the national transportation system was overhauled to improve the distribution of agricultural supplies and crops.

The results have been both good and bad. The target of self-sufficiency in food production has almost been reached, and the food shortages, so common in the 1960s, are rarer. Wheat and rice harvests have doubled with the introduction of new varieties of seeds.

The reforms have not been so successful regarding the farmers' standard of living. The new seeds need a lot of expensive chemicals and irrigation, which only the wealthier farmers can afford. Poorer farmers have run up debts to buy chemicals and equipment that they find difficult to pay off. Their quality of life has not improved; many consider themselves worse off now, especially as they have discovered that some of the new varieties of seeds cannot survive a drought and need extra irrigation, which they cannot afford to provide. Over all, the gap between rich and poor farmers has widened.

The Green Revolution has brought benefits into other parts of the Indian economy. Road and rail networks have been improved, and jobs have been created in the various new factories manufacturing agricultural chemicals. But the increased use of chemicals is alarming conservationists and doctors, who are concerned about the environment and people's health.

The Green Revolution has helped many rich farmers to buy tractors.

# 5
# Transportation, Cities, and Industries

Without water there can be no life; a nearby source of water has been the priority of all communities throughout history. So it was for the earliest people in northern India, who decided to settle alongside the Ganges because its water had many uses. People used it in their homes for drinking, washing, and cooking; for their farm animals and crops; as a source of food; even for recreation.

## An important trade route

The first settlers were hunter-gatherers who lived off the animals, fruits and plants in the thick forests that covered the plains. After the discovery of iron tools, which made it easier to clear trees for farming land, people switched to growing crops. Cattle were sacred to them, so they were only bred for their milk and to help work the land–

In Bangladesh it is easier to travel by boat than by either train or bus.

Boats carry cargoes of bricks from a brick-making factory on the riverbank near Dacca.

something that is still true today. The development of agriculture brought about the growth of other occupations and trade. As well as a source of life, the Ganges now became a natural highway along which farmers, craftsmen, and merchants traveled, opening up new villages, trades, and markets in the forest clearings on the river's banks. New ideas, too, were spread.

Changes in climate, irrigation projects, and deforestation have reduced the water level, so that long stretches of the Ganges are unnavigable. The role of the river as a transporter of goods, people, and knowledge has been taken over by roads, railroads, aircraft, television, and telecommunications. The exception is the delta, where poor road and rail networks mean that boats are still the main means of transportation. While the role of the Ganges for transportation has declined, the cities on its banks remain important: some because they are historically famous, perhaps once a military base or the capital of a powerful empire; others because of their crafts or industries; and religion or learning.

Along the upper Ganges, the most important cities are Allahabad and Kanpur; midway are Varanasi and Patna; and down near the delta are Calcutta and Dacca.

**Above** One of the few remaining textile mills in Kanpur.

**Opposite** The leather factories in Kanpur are a major source of pollution of the Ganges.

## Allahabad

People have been living in this city for thousands of years because this is one of the most sacred places in Hinduism. The city is at the meeting point of two holy rivers, the Ganges and the Yamuna, as well as the mythical Saraswati River, which is said to surface here after flowing underground from the Himalayas. The place where the rivers all join, called *sangam*, is very holy to Hindus, and thousands of pilgrims bathe here every year to wash away their sins.

Allahabad was given its present name by the great Mogul emperor Akbar in 1584. He was a Muslim and he named the city in honor of Allah (God). *Bad* means city, so Allahabad means City of God.

## Kanpur

This industrial city of two million people is sometimes called the "Manchester of India" because of its huge textile mills. The mills are still working, but the cost of modernizing the outdated machinery is causing doubts about their future. More important now is the leather industry, which turns buffalo and cow hides into clothes and shoes for export abroad: it is one of India's major money-earners. The leather industry is also the main polluter of the Ganges, discharging huge amounts of poisonous chemicals into it every day. Another important industry in Kanpur is the manufacture of guns and equipment for the Indian army, a reminder of the time when Kanpur was a British military base.

## Varanasi

Varanasi has been a center of religion, culture, and learning for more than 3,000 years. Many Hindus choose this place to have their bodies cremated—they believe it is favored by the gods. Its two electric crematoria and centuries-old burning ghats (riverside steps), with their blazing pyres of wood, are kept busy: they dispose of 40,000 corpses every year. At nearby Sarnath, the Buddha preached his first sermon on Buddhism back in the fifth century B.C. Today, tourists from all over India and the world visit this city of one million inhabitants, providing employment for many workers in hotels, restaurants, and shops. The other main industries are weaving, handicrafts, and jewelry.

Many of the workers in the silk factories of Varanasi are young children.

A busy street in Calcutta, the largest and most densely populated city in India.

32

A jute factory in Calcutta. Jute processing has been important to Calcutta for centuries.

## Patna

The remains of Pataliputra, the capital of the ancient Mauryan kingdom, have been excavated near Patna. From here, between 268 and 231 B.C., the emperor Ashoka ruled a powerful empire. Patna is less influential today and its territory is much smaller: it is the capital of the state of Bihar, one of the poorest in India, and famous for the long-grained rice grown in great quantities around it. In 1660, the tenth and last leader, or *guru*, of the Sikh religion, Govind Singh, was born here. The sacred temple, or *gurudwara*, built in his honor is one of the holiest Sikh shrines and visited by many pilgrims.

## Calcutta

With a population of 12 million, Calcutta is the largest city in India (and one of the largest in the world). Strictly speaking, Calcutta is not on the Ganges, but on the Hooghly River. It was the headquarters of the East India Company and became the capital of all the British territories in India until 1911, when the center of power was moved to New Delhi.

The city was greatly affected by the partition of India after independence from Britain in 1947: the jute farms, on which Calcutta's factories and port had thrived, now belonged to East Pakistan (the former name of Bangladesh); and millions of Hindu refugees poured over the border, fleeing from persecution in a country created specifically for Muslims.

Since then, new jute farms have been opened to supply the sixty factories in Calcutta. Although the jute industry is still a major employer, engineering has become more important in recent years. The Hooghly silts up easily, which has prevented the development of the port for large sea-going ships, so a new port is being built downstream at Haldia, next to a large oil refinery.

War between India and Pakistan, and between East and West Pakistan, has added to the refugee problem; a problem made worse by people arriving from the countryside seeking a better life in the city. It has been estimated that *at least* 100,000 people live and sleep on the streets of Calcutta. In addition, 4 million people live in cramped, one-room dwellings, often flooded by the yearly monsoon rains.

## Dacca

Once the chief city of the Indian state of East Bengal, Dacca became the capital of East Pakistan when Pakistan was created after Indian independence. Dissatisfied with the way it was treated by West Pakistan, the East broke away in 1971 to become Bangladesh. Today, the country's defenselessness in the face of natural disasters, caused by its position near the mouths of the Ganges and Brahmaputra rivers, and its enormous population, make Dacca the capital of one of the poorest nations in the world. Bangladesh is heavily dependent on agriculture, with few industries, most of which are concentrated around Dacca. The main industries manufacture cement, brick, and steel.

**Right** A crowded sidewalk in the heart of Dacca, the capital of Bangladesh.

### The East India Company
This was a trading company formed in 1600 by the British government to take part in the spice trade in the East Indies in Southeast Asia. After being driven out of the islands by Dutch colonists, the company developed trade with India. The East India Company became involved in politics, acting for the British government from the eighteenth to mid-nineteenth century.
Following a revolt of the Indian troops in 1857, sometimes known as the Indian Mutiny, power was transferred from the East India Company to the British government, and the Company ceased to exist in 1874.
The Writers Building in Calcutta (*below*) was once the head office of the East India Company.

34

# 6
# The Polluted River

## India's sewer

For most of history, people all over the world have abused rivers, taking the fresh water and replacing it with their own waste. Regrettably, the Indians' treatment of the Ganges is no exception to this behavior.

Over the centuries, as cities and industries developed along its banks, the river became steadily more filthy. Recent surveys estimate that 275 million gallons of liquid waste are discharged every day into the Ganges—much of it untreated, raw sewage and harmful industrial chemicals. Warnings about the consequences were ignored until the early 1980s, by which time the Ganges resembled an enormous sewer. Where once the river's waters had been a source of life, they now carried bacteria and poisons capable of causing death.

Untreated domestic and industrial waste flows from this village into the Ganges.

As part of the Ganges Action Plan, the Netherlands government is helping to build waste-treatment plants in Kanpur to reduce the amount of chemicals being discharged into the Ganges.

## Cleaning up the Ganges

A massive clean-up program, the Ganges Action Plan (GAP), was started by the Indian Government in 1985. It had two distinct aims.

First, there needed to be a considerable reduction in the amount of untreated waste pouring into the river from factories and homes.

Second, with the help of widespread publicity, the GAP was to make the population aware of the dangers of pollution so that people would have more respect for the environment and for the condition of the river.

To achieve the first aim, the Indian government has turned to Western countries, particularly Britain and the Netherlands, for assistance. Together,

they are building water-treatment plants to purify liquid waste before it is dumped in the river. One problem is that few Indian homes have bathrooms, nor are there many public restrooms for the people to use. Instead they make use of the banks of the Ganges. The government cannot afford to provide bathrooms in every home but more public toilets are being built, and sewage systems are being improved so that the amount of raw waste flowing directly into the river is far less than it was at one time.

Another issue being tackled is a sensitive religious one, for the GAP has been challenging some of the centuries-old funeral customs of Hinduism. After death, devout Hindus are cremated on the banks of the Ganges and have their

This treatment plant at Varanasi prevents raw sewage from draining into the river.

Traditional Hindu funeral pyres on the riverbank at Patna.

ashes scattered over the river. If the corpses are burned properly, this is no problem, but many people cannot afford to buy enough wood for a funeral pyre, so half-burned bodies end up in the river. Very poor people often throw their relatives' bodies straight into the water. Furthermore, according to Hindu customs, the corpses of children under eleven years old, priests, and adults who have died from certain diseases are also placed directly in the river. The result of all these practices is that a decaying body in the Ganges is an everyday sight. The government is encouraging people to use the electric crematoria that have been built in cities like Varanasi and Calcutta. However, although these are

## Rajiv Kapur

"I started the pressure group, Environment India, to draw attention to pollution in Kanpur and in the Ganges River. In Kanpur the leather tanneries dump thousands of gallons of poisonous chemicals into the river every day. But the leather industry provides jobs for 65,000 workers and also earns a lot of money. So no one wants to upset the factory owners by demanding the installation of expensive treatment plants. We can't go on like this forever, otherwise there will be nothing left for our grandchildren. Environment India is opening people's eyes and minds, so there is hope for a better tomorrow."

cheaper than a traditional wood pyre, people are reluctant to change their ways, even though this will help clean up the river and save trees.

Work is now in progress in twenty-seven Indian towns and cities all along the length of the river. The water quality is regularly checked by taking samples of it for testing in laboratories. Already these tests have shown noticeable improvements in the river's cleanliness.

Educating people, with the help of various exhibitions, discussions, and competitions, has made the population more aware of the issues involved and how they can help to improve the situation.

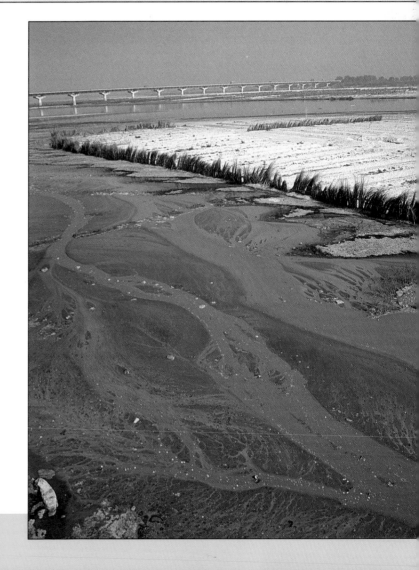

Poisonous factory waste clogs up the Ganges near Kanpur.

# 7

# The Sacred River

## The Ganges is born

The religion of most people in India is Hinduism. One of its many myths concerns the creation of the Ganges. Far back in time, northern India was ruled by King Sagar, proud father of 60,000 sons! These youths, so the story goes, were so disrespectful to Kapil Muni, a seaside holy man, that he reduced them to ashes with a withering look.

When the distraught king turned to the gods for help, they replied that his sons would be brought back to life only if their sinful remains were cleansed by the waters of the goddess Ganga, a river then residing in the heavens. After much praying and pleading by another holy man, Bhagirath, Ganga reluctantly consented to descend to earth. To break her fall, the god Shiva stepped in the way and let the river tumble gently though his long hair onto the Himalayas. Ganga then flowed across India to the edge of the ocean, where she washed over the ashes and restored King Sagar's sons to life—an event commemorated every January with a festival on Sagar Island, at the mouth of the Hooghly River. This ceremony is attended by hundreds of thousands of Hindu pilgrims from all over India.

Journey's end: pilgrims bathing during the annual festival on Sagar Island, at the point where the Ganges enters the Bay of Bengal.

## The holy water

This mythical story explains why Hindus have always respected the river—a river often described by them as *Parabrahmasvarupini*: the "Embodiment of the Supreme Spirit," who is called Brahma, the creator of the universe. The Ganges represents one of the many gods and goddesses of Hinduism. In the same way that they pray to a statue of a god in a temple, Hindus pray to the river, asking the goddess Ganga for her blessing and her forgiveness. If they live alongside the river, their worship will involve bathing in it twice a day, at dawn and dusk, and offering the river gifts of flowers and food. Devout Hindus will make an effort to attend a festival at one of the many sacred places on the river.

Pilgrims from all over India come to the Ganges to collect and take home some of its holy water.

### Bolegiri

"I am a sadhu, which means holy man. A sadhu chooses to spend his life thinking about god and religion instead of having a job, home, and family. In India, people don't think this is unusual, so there are many sadhus. Like me, most of them wear orange-colored clothes, the sacred color of Hinduism. The markings on my forehead show that I am a follower of the god Shiva. I spend my life visiting all the sacred places on the Ganges, as well as the other shrines in India dedicated to Shiva. Besides a blanket and a small bag, I have no possessions. I eat and sleep in temples and hostels and people pay for my rail and bus tickets."

41

Afterward, they will take home a container of its water to use in religious ceremonies.

Whatever distance they travel or however they keep it, the water will always remain fresh. This is one of the peculiar properties of the Ganges that has never been satisfactorily explained: something in the water kills off harmful bacteria, so that it is free of the germs that turn it stale and spread diseases. However, in recent years the water has become so polluted that scientists doubt whether the Ganges is capable of keeping itself pure. They have started the campaign to clean up the river, which is discussed in the previous chapter. But no matter how filthy it appears to Western eyes, millions of Hindus continue to bathe in it, convinced that their river goddess will do them no harm and will, in fact, bring them good luck and a long and healthy life.

### The Ganges Is Good for You—Fact or Faith?

Like most of the world's rivers, just looking at the Ganges is enough to deter you from swimming in it or drinking its water. Yet thousands of Indians do this everyday and survive, even downstream of the poisonous pollution from Kanpur's leather factories. Do they build up a resistance or is there really something in the water that keeps it germ-free?

Some scientists say that medicinal herbs in the mountains are responsible for this trait. Geologists maintain it is the radioactive minerals in the rocky sediment from the Himalayas. Whatever the reason, the Ganges' ability to clean itself is a fact. However, even if the river can rid itself of harmful bacteria, it is extremely unlikely that it can cancel out life-threatening chemicals so that they are safe to drink. It is the rapid increase in the levels of these poisons in the river that has forced the government to take steps to control the waste that is dumped in the Ganges.

The evening Aarti ceremony at Hardwar in honor of the goddess Ganga.

# 8
# The Years Ahead

More water now flows under Calcutta's Howrah Bridge, as a result of the building of the Farakka Dam in India.

Now 25 million years old—even older according to Hindu mythology—the Ganges has had a turbulent history. The river has witnessed the rise and fall of powerful empires; the spread of important religions, ideas, and trade; the widespread destruction of forests and their replacement with cities and factories that have choked its waters with their waste products; and the devastating impact of the weather on people along its banks.

But what of the future? Can the people of the Ganges' basin look forward to better times? It would be very difficult to reassure these people, especially as it is already too late to restore the damage that was begun years ago. The most serious damage is the deforestation in Nepal, on India's northern border. Even if this were stopped right now, it would take years to restore. The damage has been done, and Bangladesh, the country most affected, could do nothing to stop it.

## The Consequences of Deforestation

In the early 1940s, 60 percent of Nepal was covered in forest. There was enough land to grow crops for food for the 5 million people who lived there and trees were replaced at the same rate as they were chopped down for firewood. By the 1980s, the population had grown to 20 million, increasing the demand for wood and farmland so much that only 30 percent of Nepal remained forest. Now 310 sq. mi. of trees are being destroyed every year, less than 50 sq. mi. are replanted.

Without a protective covering of vegetation to lessen the impact of the monsoon, nor roots to hold the soil, huge quantities of hillside soil are swept by the rains into rivers. The Ganges and the Brahmaputra together carry two billion tons of sediment to the sea, more than any other river system in the world. The sediment blocks up rivers, reducing their flow and making them more likely to flood. At the delta there is less fresh water flowing out to meet the salty sea water brought in by the tides, and force it back out to sea. This salty water is creeping farther up the channels and ruining good farmland. The photograph (*below*) shows the effects of deforestation in Nepal.

Bangladesh, too, has been harmed by a decision of the Indian government. The Farakka Dam, just inside the Indian border, was built by India to increase the flow of water in the Hooghly River during the dry winter months, to prevent the port of Calcutta from silting up. Inevitably, the dam has altered the amount of water going into Bangladesh.

Now the country's rivers are clogging up faster than ever with sediment and the farmers of Bangladesh have less water for irrigation, at a time when they most need it. Both countries have been in dispute for many years, with Bangladesh accusing India of keeping back too much water, and India disagreeing.

A satisfactory solution must be found soon, especially as Bangladesh's river system will be disrupted even more if India carries out plans to transfer water from the Ganges and Brahmaputra to rivers in the south through a network of canals.

Looking even further into the future, India and its neighboring countries are desperately short of electricity and demand for it is rising all the time. The best way of providing it would be to harness the power of the fast-flowing rivers in the Himalayas, but can all the countries involved—Nepal, China, India, and Bangladesh—agree on how it should be done and how the electricity should be shared? Only time will tell.

**Left** Constant dredging of the Hooghly, to remove the silt brought down by the river, enables container ships to dock in Calcutta.

**Right** High above the Alaknanda River, this Himalayan resort gets its electricity from the sun.

# Glossary

**Alluvium** Fertile soil that has been formed from all the material deposited by a river.

**Bacteria** Tiny living cells that are sometimes harmful.

**Buddha** A nobleman and religious teacher from northern India who founded the religion of Buddhism.

**Caste** A social group or class of people in India.

**Colonists** People who go to another country to settle there.

**Crematoria** Buildings where dead bodies are cremated, or burned.

**Cyclone** A fierce storm with high winds and heavy rain.

**Decade** A period of ten years.

**Deforestation** The destruction of large areas of trees.

**Delta** A flat, fan-shaped area where a river splits into many channels at the end of its course.

**Drought** A long period without rain.

**Environment** The surroundings in which humans, plants, and animals live, which influence their development and behavior.

**Epicenter** The point at which tremors from inside the earth reach the surface and cause earthquakes.

**Erode** To wear away.

**Famine** A severe shortage of food when many people do not have enough to eat.

**Geological** Connected to geology, the study of the earth's rocks, soils, etc.

**Ghat** Steps or a landing place on a riverbank.

**Global warming** The increase in the average temperatures of the earth, caused by the build-up of gases in the atmosphere that slow down the escape of the sun's heat from the earth.

**Habitat** The natural home of an animal or plant.

**Hinduism** The main religion in India. Its followers are called Hindus.

**Irrigation** Supplying land with water through canals, ditches, etc.

**Jute** A plant, the fibers of which are used to make sacks and ropes.

**Mangrove** A tree with long roots hanging from its trunk, usually found in marshy areas near the sea.

**Mauryan kingdom** A kingdom ruled by powerful rulers in the third and second centuries B.C. During this time a great civilization flowered in India.

**Meander** To take a winding course.

**Meteorologist** People who study the weather.

**Mogul emperor** A ruler of a Muslim empire that covered large parts of India from the sixteenth to eighteenth centuries.

**Monsoon** Summer winds that bring rain to much of India and Bangladesh. The word is also used to describe the rainy season.

**Muslim** Someone who follows the teachings of the Prophet Muhammad.

**Mythology** A collection of myths or stories about heroes or gods of ancient times.

**Navigable** Able to be used by boats or ships.

**Nutrients** Food that plants and animals need to help them grow.

**Partition of India** The division of the Indian subcontinent into India and Pakistan, after India achieved independence from British rule in 1947.

**Pesticides** Chemicals that kill pests which are harmful to plants.

**Pyre** A pile of wood for a cremation.

**Rapids** Sections of a river where the water is churned up by strong currents or rocks.

**Refugees** People who are forced to leave their homes because of war, disaster, or poverty.

**River basin** The area that is drained by a large river and all its tributaries.

**Salinity** The amount of salt in water: it is high in sea water and low in river water.

**Sediment** All the material, such as sand, gravel, stones, and earth, that is carried by a river and deposited on its bed, at its delta, or on its banks when it floods.

**Self-sufficiency** The ability to supply all your own needs.
**Sikh** A follower of Sikhism, a religion founded in India in the sixteenth century.
**Silt** Very fine mud or clay carried by a river.
**Spiritual** Concerned with religion.
**Subsistence farming** When most of the produce is consumed by the farmer and his family, leaving little or nothing to be sold for income.
**Terrain** An area of land. This word is used to describe what an area is like; for example "rocky terrain."
**Tributaries** Small rivers that flow into a larger one.
**Vulnerable** To be exposed to danger.

# Books to Read and Useful Addresses

To find out more about the issues discussed in this book, try to get some of these books from your library.

Ardley, Brigette and Neil. *India.* Silver Burdett Press, 1989
Caldwell, John C. *India.* Chelsea House, 1990
Author not listed. *India.* Marshall Cavendish, 1991
Cumming, David. *India.* Watts, 1989
McNair, Sylvia. *India.* Childrens, 1990
Nugent, Nicholas. *India.* Steck-Vaughn, 1991
Rowland-Entwistle, Theodore. *Rivers and Lakes.* Silver Burdett Press, 1987

More advanced readers will find the following books interesting:

Aitken, Bill. *Seven Sacred Rivers.* Penguin, 1992

Darian, Steven G. *Ganges in Myth and History.* University of Hawaii Press, 1978
Dennison, Berwick. *A Walk Along the Ganges.* Century, 1986
Frater, Alexander. *Chasing the Monsoon.* Penguin, 1991
Gole, Susan. *India Within the Ganges.* South Asia Books, 1983

**Addresses**
Indian Tourist Office
30 Rockefeller Plaza North
New York, NY 10112

For first-hand knowledge about cleaning up the Ganges you could write to :
Environment India,
18 M.I.G. Rattan Lal Nagar, Kanpur, India.

**Picture acknowledgments**
All photographs including the cover are by David Cumming except the following:
Bruce Coleman/Gerald Cubitt 10 (top), /Erwin and Peggy Bauer 14, /J. Zwaenepoel 25, /John Murray 44; Hutchison Library 15, /S. Dent 19 (lower); Wayland Picture Library/Jimmy Holmes 21 (top), 27. The map on page 5 is by Peter Bull Design. Artwork on pages 6, 9, and 16 are by John Yates.
The author would like to thank Sandeep Chadda and the staff of *The Pioneer* newspaper in Kanpur and Tribhuvan Signh Chauhan for their help.

# INDEX